MW00717797

Employment Survival Manual

How to Find a Job in Las Vegas
2004/2005

Robert Saunders

Llumina Press

Copyright 2004 Robert Saunders.

All rights reserved. No part of this publication may be reproduced or trans-
mitted in any form or by any means electronic or mechanical, including
photocopy, recording, or any information storage and retrieval system, without permission in writing from both the copyright owner and the publisher.

Requests for permission to make copies of any part of this work should be
mailed to Permissions Department, Llumina Press, P.O. Box 772246, Coral
Springs, FL 33077-2246.

ISBN: 1-59526-320-9
Printed in the United States of America by Llumina Press.

Table of Contents

Introduction

This book is designed to prepare you mentally, physically and spiritually to be successful at obtaining a job, today, now, in the city of Las Vegas, Nevada.

It is designed to give you both a general understanding and overview of today's Las Vegas job market and specific tools, knowledge and understanding of what is required to find work.

It is meant to be a practical work leading to a job. For this reason you will find the overview of the Las Vegas job market at the end of the book and not at the beginning.

It is also a literal work and if you take it literally you will find success in your job search. It is completely based upon actual day-to-day experience in the job market. All of the things which it describes are both true and accurate and, again, should be followed as stated. The attitudes and methods described here work, so please try and be as faithful to them as you can be.

You will also note that some sections cover material that you will also find in other sections. Each of the major areas are meant to be stand-alone chapters so you will not have to read the entire book if you are only interested in one area. For example, if you are just interested in a job at a hotel and casino, you will not have to read chapters about other areas. However, I strongly suggest that you take the time to read the whole book before you begin.

The two most important things to remember about getting a job are:

1. do everything right the first time;
2. the sooner you start the faster you will find work.

Chapter One

O.K., You Are in Las Vegas and You Need a Job.

Who are you?

It is important to remember that this book is for the average person, for the hundreds of thousands of everyday people in Las Vegas who need to find work. If you are a highly sought after professional, this book is not for you.

If, on the other hand, you have worked for the last however many years for a company or industry which no longer exists or from which you have been laid off, if you have been unable to work for some reason for the past X years and now wish to re-enter the labor market, if you have just graduated from high school, or didn't graduate and are ready to find your first job, if you were injured or have a disability and can now work again, if you just moved here in hopes of a better, or at least a warmer life and need to find a way to support your family or yourself, if you are retired and want a job to have something to do, or you are the former CEO of a company who suddenly finds him or herself stranded in the desert for personal reasons beyond your control and you just need to survive until your spaceship lands, then this book is MUST reading for you. This book will not tell you how to become president of the MGM Grand. If you have to read a book, any book, to tell you how to go about it, then you are not qualified by definition. This will not tell you how to get one of the high-powered jobs at a casino or other Vegas industry, for the same reason. But it will tell you how to get a job - how to get a job and survive in the unusual community that is Las Vegas, Nevada.

Now that you find yourself in need of a job here in Las Vegas, the first thing you have to do for yourself is define in clear terms who you are. By this I mean what you have done, can do, are willing to do and, very importantly, why you need a job.

Why you need a job

On the face of it this may seem like a really silly question and I can hear many people shouting, "For money you idiot!" Well, though it is true that all work involves the earning of money, money is not always the motivating factor or most important factor in wanting to work. Being able to have a clear understanding and definition of who you are and why you want to work, is instrumental in determining what kind of job you will begin to look for. The distinction is this: do you want a job or do you need a job? There is a major difference between the two. People who want a job may not need a job, whereas people who need a job may not want a job. Sounds crazy? Well it's not, and you must be able to give yourself an honest assessment in this regard.

You want a job

As stated before, a person who wants a job may or may not need a job. This is important because want is not nearly as powerful a motivator as need.

A person who wants a job but does not need a job is basically someone whose day-to-day existence is not immediately threatened by not having a job. A person just graduating from or leaving high school who has well-to-do loving parents may not "need" a job. His parents may not care if he works right away or ever and he will always have food shelter and clothing (not to mention a car, a cell phone and a girl/boy friend who wants to go out). These persons may decide for whatever reason that they want to get a job. Their school counselor tells them they should be independent and find a job; their less fortunate friends get jobs, they want to impress someone, they are bored and want something to do, etc., but their motivation is low. Why? Because they don't need a job! The walk from unemployment to employment is a long and slow one for them, or at least it can be. It is true that this person may be the next mega rock star or Bill Gates waiting to emerge and eager to get to work and make it, but typically this is not the case.

A person who wants to work may be a retired person who is just tired of being at home. They may seek the social environment of work and the fun of being around other people. If they find something to do, great, but if they don't, it's also great. Or it could be someone receiving disability benefits substantial enough for them to maintain their current life style. A person receiving $1800 a month in SSDI payments is not likely to take an $8 dollar an hour job ($1200 a month before taxes). Or the person may have survivor benefits or one of many other forms of support that allows them to be happy where they are. The list, of course, is much longer than this but the point is that people in these situations, though they may like to work, don't really need to work and this difference can have a profound effect on their job search efforts.

This can manifest itself in many ways. They can be very picky about what they want to do and when they want to do it. They just can't work on Tuesday and Thursday and they are happy to wait as long as it takes to find a job that accommodates them. This can be difficult in a reality where employees accommodate employers and not the other way around. They may want to make more money than they are qualified to make and set a dollar goal that is unrealistic for them or even for the employment community where they live, and again they may be perfectly willing to wait until someone knocks on their door and offers them $20 an hour before considering working, though they would love to work for $20 an hour. They may decide they need more training and decide that going back to school, not working, is the thing to do. Whatever the case, they are not highly motivated to go out and find work.

You need a job

The person who "needs" a job is, or at least should be, a highly motivated person. The person who needs a job cannot afford to be very picky. This person wants to do something that he/she can do and something that he/she likes to do, if possible; but their job search is not motivated by their wants, it is motivated by their needs. If he/she cannot find a job in a chosen or preferred area, he/she still needs a job and must find a job. After discovering that there are no immediate jobs in the areas of his/her wants, he/she is willing to find a job that wants him/her, not one that he/she wants. Money and survival are the motivating factors here.

Another example: a person has been laid off, the unemployment money is going to run out in two weeks; he/she has not found the job they have been looking for, but they know they must have income within the next two weeks or their house of cards will fall down. They have phone, power and rent bills, a family to support, food to buy, they need gas for the car. They have only themselves to depend on but others are depending on them. They need a job and they need a job now.

It is important to note, in the above example, that this does not mean this person should lose all hope or interest in finding the job they would like to have - it doesn't. It just means that they have to be able to survive while they continue the search for that job. It is also important to remember that in today's world, whether you want or need a job, the job that you get is not likely to be the last job you will ever have. But the person who needs a job, typically really needs a job now. He/she needs gas, food, shelter, the whole nine yards and cannot afford to drop the ball. When they find themselves at that point, where they have done their best to find the job that they want but have not found, when their dead line is up, they then need to find the job that wants them.

This person is highly motivated, he's looking for work everyday and wants to do as much as possible to improve his chances of finding work. This person cannot afford not to read this book.

Now you have to be honest with yourself and determine who you are. Do you want a job or need one? The answer to this question will determine how you conduct your job search.

If you want a job, even a voluntary position may do for you. Having something to do in the company of other people with like interests may be just what you need. If you simply want a job, you can prepare a resume and send one out to every job doing what you want to do and sit back and wait for the results. (As an aside let me point out that in Las Vegas 99% of all resumes sent out do not get answered. This means that if you send out 100 resumes in a month you might only receive one response and it may just say no thank you.) If you need a job you will plan your job search around the jobs that are most available at any given time. You will tailor your search around what employers want that your background and abilities say you can do.

Again remember, this job you are now looking for does not define the rest of your life, it is not who you are and it is not the last job you will look for or have. In fact if you are in the 'need a job' category it may simply be a method to survive, a part one of your plan to continue searching for the job you really want and will prosper in.

Chapter Two

How to begin looking for a job

So, for whatever reason you need a job, how do you start looking for one?

The best way to begin is to ask your friends and family if they know of any available jobs. The truth is that nepotism is king when it comes to employment, not just in Las Vegas, but anywhere in the world. So if you have a relative or a friend who owns a company or runs a company or who is in position to hire or refer to a company, don't be shy about asking them for help. This is especially true in Las Vegas, because Las Vegas is what's referred to as a good-old boy kind of a place. Simply put, this translates into who you know is a heck of a lot more important than what you know.

Remember Vegas is a town where two thirds of the population is new, so if you know somebody, or even think that you know somebody, give them a call.

The next best place to begin is with the Sunday newspaper. Note that I said newspaper not newspapers, as I would have said just about any place else. This is because basically we only have one paper here in town, which again is an indication of how narrow the range of possibilities really are.

Of course you could look at the employment section of the newspaper on any day, but Sunday is the only one worth spending time with. Sunday is the day when all of the employers place their ads. If you have a computer at home, search the LVRJ (Las Vegas Review Journal) on line. For one thing it's free, for another you can search section by section according to your interest and you can have the type as big or small as you want. Believe it or not, being comfortable while you read the papers for a job is very important. This is because fighting with a paper and struggling with print that may be a tad small for you is quite tiring and creates an obstacle to looking for a job, right from the start, that you don't need. Of course if you don't have a computer, the regular old newspaper will do.

If you are one of those lucky people who has a profession and knows exactly what you are looking for, great. Remember, chances are, if you are a seasoned professional with a stunning resume, this book is not for you. This book, as stated before, is for the average person looking to make an honest living or the seasoned professional who, for whatever reason, find themselves in the disturbing position of not having any recourse in their profession and having to start over again. In either of these cases look at everything one section at a time, going from things that seem interesting to you to things you think you could do or even hate to do; give yourself a good idea of what's available.

Get the paper as soon as it comes out in your area of town. Go to wherever you buy the Sunday paper, or plan to buy it, and find out when is the earliest it is available. Be there and try and get the first one. Don't be shy about using the phone or the fax on Sunday. When you find something interesting, if there is a number, call and find out about it. If there is only a fax number and you want more information about the job, fax in a request. If there is no number, but just the name of the company, look up the number and call. If you have a resume and you think it fits the prospect, fax it on Sunday. If there is a number or you get the number, call on Monday morning to confirm that your resume was received. But whatever you do, remember that you are in Las Vegas, so don't take no response to your resume personally.

After you have found a few things in your primary area of interest (if you do) and you have faxed in your resume, don't stop there. Find a secondary group of possibilities and fax a resume to them also. Realistically you will need more than one resume. You will need to tweak your resume to highlight your strengths and experience to fit the individual job you are applying for.

If you don't have a resume, get one. In the workbook section at the end of this book you will find help in compiling the information needed to make a resume if you don't already know how. But remember a resume is not just information; it is also presentation and style. There are many sources of information on creating a good resume, or consider hiring someone to do it for you. Not all jobs require resumes, but no employer is averse to receiving one, so having one is important.

Other good sources of employment information are online job banks, like monster.com and many others. Your local unemployment office has job postings. Local, state or federal agencies and programs like NV job link, NV Business services and others have extensive job listings available both posted in their offices and on computer. If you don't have a computer, many of these places, including the public library, have computers available for your use.

Hitting the pavement is also a wonderful source of direct possibilities. Visit the human resources or personnel departments of companies that interest you. You will find that quite often there are many positions available that are not advertised frequently or at all. Go to the HR departments at the hotel and casino of your choice and if you don't find something right away, go to all of them. This is also true of major retailers and state and government departments. If you do even half of the things mentioned above, you will discover that there are a vast number of jobs to find and apply for.

In order to be effective, you will have to have a method to your madness. You will need to structure your search and your follow-up. The key to this is to develop a search routine and to keep an accurate log of your efforts.

Looking for a job is work. It may in fact be harder work than the job you eventually find. For this reason you have to treat it like work and have a search schedule, just as you have a work schedule. Plan to get the paper as early as possible Sunday or Saturday night if possible. What happens next more or less depends on your energy level. Some people will be able to go over the entire employment section in one day or less, other people may require more time. But the point is to take as much time as you need but take it consistently. So when you get the paper, plan to spend X amount of time with it each day until you have finished it. As an example, spend an hour a day on your job search.

Your first mission is to find jobs that seem interesting to you and make a list of them. The first time around don't be too picky, just copy anything that looks promising. How you do this depends on what tools you have available. Of course it is easier to do it with a computer. Simply copy the listings and paste them into a word processing program. If you don't have a computer or access to a computer, do it by hand. Circle the listings as you find them, and then making sure that you don't destroy listings on the back of the page you are working on, cut them out and scotch tape them into a note book. Remember to put the date of the paper on the page with the listings. Again you might be able to do this in an hour; if so great, but if not, just do it as best you can.

This will be your first draft of that week's listings. Go over it and circle or highlight the listings in order of interest to you. Put a number one in the most interesting and go from there (or use different colors of highlighter). Once this is done, begin faxing resumes or calling, depending on the instructions in the listing.

You will be faxing out a cover letter and a resume. Keep copies of the cover letters with notes as to when you faxed them out. If you send out more than one form of resume, put a note on the saved cover letter as to which resume you sent.

As the days and weeks go by you will be able to see if the ads you responded to are still listed and on which week they stopped being listed. You will know when you faxed them and how many times. If you get a response, find the appropriate cover letter and make a note on it. As you get interviews, do the same, noting how you felt about them. As you do this you will learn a lot about the employers advertising in the paper by noting when, if and how long it took them to respond and how long and often they run ads.

This will also allow you to know when the same employers list new ads. Look in the daily papers as well to see if there are new ads listed. If you are beginning your Sunday routine and you see a job that looks just perfect, interrupt your routine and just fax them right away, the sooner you get your information to them the better. Afterwards, continue with your search as usual.

Your job search logbooks should also include any other leads you find, either from a job-link office or from friends or family. Being businesslike about it will keep you centered and make you more determined to get a job so you can stop working so hard just looking for one.

Chapter Three

The Interview – The Application

THE INTERVIEW

The interview is where the tire meets the road in job hunting. It's where you come face to face with your prospective employer and have the daunting task of showing him, that of all the people who are applying for the same job that you want, he should choose you. How do you do this? How do you make yourself stand out in a crowd of people who all want the same thing? Ultimately the answer is you must simply do the best you can. But many people miss the mark by failing to realize that doing the best they can may not be simple. You have to prepare for an interview, not just show up for it. Here in Las Vegas, this one thing alone will separate you from 90% of your competitors. So, how do you prepare for an interview?

I look at preparing for an interview in two ways. There is the nuts and bolts preparation; the work and facts that must be done, and the spiritual preparation, the attitude and mindset that you need to have when you sit down with your interviewer.

The good thing about the nuts and bolts aspect of preparing for your interview is that 1) the elements required are always the same and 2) once you have put it all together, you don't have to do it again.

THE APPLICATION

You have to compose your complete work history for at least the past ten years. Ten years is the magic number here because our largest employer, the hotel and casino industry requires it. These are the elements that are required in a complete work history. First of all you must list "every" job you have had in this period of time. "Every" job means every job literally, no matter if you only had the job for one day. If you received a paycheck for it (which means it was reported to the IRS), then you must list this job, as it will be part of your social security work history. If you are a young person, this may be very easy, as you may have had only one or two jobs or less, if you are just out of school.

For an older person, this could be quite a task, especially if you have had many jobs in many states (which is not unusual here in the ever-changing town of Las Vegas). One of the many difficulties for the older person may be something as simple, yet as deadly important, as remembering every little job that he/she has had. Ten years can be a long time. But this must be done because failing to remember just one little part time job that you had six years ago can cost you a job you would otherwise have gotten. This is particularly true within the hotel and casino industry because they are required to run extensive background checks on their employees. To protect themselves, they generally take this very seriously and have strict standards of compliance, one of which is that all employment be listed.

If their backgrounds check turns up even one part-time job that was not listed on your application, you are generally declined by default, no matter what your other qualifications are and no matter how much the manager of your future department may have wanted to hire you. Unfortunately the reason for the decline is almost never revealed to you and you don't get a second chance, so you have to have it right the very first time. Please remember this, make a note, you only get one chance, it has to be right the very first time.

Our young job seeker, as noted, does not have an issue with this generally, but how is our older, typical, job seeker, who has had many jobs, perhaps in many states, to make sure his memory is correct?

Actually the answer is quite simple. For an hour or so of your time and $35.00 you can go to your nearest social security office and ask for a print out of your ten-year work history. You just need your social security card and $35.00. Typically they will print one out for you on the spot. This printout represents your "official" work history and is the same work history that any employer will receive. So by getting it, you will have made sure that every job for which you have ever been paid (legally) will be on your employment application. However these printouts are a little hard to read so you will have to study them carefully to make sense of them. They also do not include all the information you will need about each job listed to fill out your application, but at least you will know for what jobs you have to fill in information.

Now that you have your complete work history you can begin to fill out your application. All applications ask for basically the same information.

1. **Name of employer.** This appears on your printout.
2. **Address of employer.** If you worked for a national chain of some sort, be it a Home Depot or Burger King, the address listed on your print out may be for a corporate office and not the actual location where you worked. If this is the case, you need to get the address of your location. You may have to look it up and call them.
3. **Telephone number of the employer.** This will not be on the printout; you will have to look it up and give them a valid phone number. They will not look it up for you and if the number you give them is not good, your application will die.
4. **The name of your supervisor.** Usually a first name alone will do, but if you have a last name also, of course include it. If it is a job where you worked nine years ago, or a job you worked for only one week, there is a good chance you will not remember your supervisor's name. Don't worry too much about this, the conventional wisdom is to just put down any first name, male or female. As long as the phone number is good you should be O.K.
5. **The dates that you worked for the company**. This has to be exact, at least to the month and year. You cannot just say from 1995 to 1998, you have to say from 12/95 to 3/98, and it has to be accurate. Just as with listing every job, if you list incorrect employment dates your application will be automatically declined. You will be able to get the years that you worked for a company from your 10-year printout but not the months; you will have to call each company to get this information if you don't remember it.
6. **Your starting and ending salaries**. Again, this information will have to be correct; it does not appear on your print out and you will have to call the company to get the information if you do not remember it.

7. **Your job title**. Again this information must be correct. If you list one job title and the employer gives another, your application will be dropped.

8. **A description of your job duties.** In most cases your job title will tell what you did, but use this section as an opportunity to give them an idea of your abilities. Also use this section to include things that may not be indicated by your job title. As an example, if you were a custodian and you are applying for a job as a floor cleaner, mention that you stripped and waxed floors as a part of your job duties.

9. **Can they contact your former employers?** Of course, the answer is yes. The only exception may be your current employer, if contacting them may cause you to lose your present job before you are hired for a new job. Just tell them this and typically they will agree to contact them only after they have decided to hire you.

10. **Why did you leave your last job**? This is a very important question, so do not take it lightly. There must be a good acceptable reason. This could be almost anything, you got a better job, you wanted to try something new, you got laid off, etc. If you were fired, it is always a judgment call as to whether or not you should say that or try something softer, like you got laid off. Generally I always advise not to make or give negative responses, but what's true is true, though sometimes you can bend the truth a little to help you along. I cannot advise you to lie, but I can point out to you that Las Vegas is a right-to-work state and one of the provisions of this is that a former employer cannot tell a prospective new employer that they fired you. They, technically, can only say that they would not hire you again, so it's your call. Be careful about medical reasons for leaving jobs. It you had a medical reason be sure that it is something that has now been resolved and will not give the appearance of possibly affecting the position you are applying for. Though it does not appear on the application, you will be asked if you gave your former employers notice before you moved on to your new job. Always say yes, no matter what the case actually was.

Other items in the nuts and bolts category are punctuality, personal hygiene and interview attire. Surprisingly, it is not apparent to everyone that being on time is very important. So much so that you should make a point of being at any interview at least 15 minutes early. Remember, it is better to be "an hour early than a minute late"; this applies equally well when you have a job but twice that when you are still looking for one.

Personal hygiene is very important. This may sound like an unnecessary point to mention but sometimes people simply overlook it for whatever reason. Make sure that you shower or bathe before your interview. Make sure you use a good deodorant. Make sure you brush your teeth and be sure to take breath mints of some kind with you. Check your breath just before your interview and use a breath mint if necessary; in fact, use one anyway before your interview. Make sure your hair is clean and well groomed. I realize that this may go against the grain of many, but if you want a job it is best to appear as "normal" as possible and even though some of us may deny knowing what this means, we all do. But just in case, this would mean such things as removing excessive jewelry for women and removing all face jewelry for men. No nose rings or earrings for men. No visible piercing or other decorative artifacts. Men should be clean-shaven and their hair should be conservative.

Interview attire

If you have time before you start your job search go to any personal or human resources office at one of our hotel casinos and look at the people filling out applications. You will notice typically, that 95% plus of the people there are dressed too casually. In jeans, in tee shirts, or they have their shirts out of their pants or are wearing sneakers or sandals or they may have hats of some sort. The point of this is to show you just how easy it is to stand out in an interview or application situation simply by dressing appropriately.!

This is Las Vegas and because of the heat, typical attire here is casual, so no one requires that you wear a suit and tie to an interview, although there are positions for which they are absolutely necessary. Most of the positions, which the average person here will be applying for, do not necessitate it. But it is important to look "business" casual and not "playing-football-in-the-street" casual. You should not wear blue jeans, tee shirts or sneakers, period. Just about any pair of "not jeans" pants will do. A clean and pressed pair of cotton pants of any type will do, but they should have belt loops and you must wear a belt. Any shirt with a collar will do, as long as it is clean and pressed. This means anything from a golf shirt to a button-up shirt. Whatever your choice of shirt it should be a solid color. Any solid color isO.K., but try to stay away from colors that blind the eyes. Any pair of "not sneaker" shoes will also do, as long as they are clean and polished. If you happen to have a nice sport coat or jacket, wearing it would be a nice touch, but it is not mandatory as the other things are. Of course it is important that whatever you wear fits you properly. No giant baggy pants, no pants falling off of your hips.

For women, no matter how attractive and sexy you may be, please do not wear sexy clothes to your interview. Skirts and dresses should be conservative and the length should be close to either side of your knees.

Cologne for men and perfume for women is fine, but in moderation only.

You will be amazed to find that a simple pair of pants, a nice simple shirt and a plain pair of shoes will make you look professional and stand you out from the crowd.

Spiritual preparation, mindset and attitude

Looking decent is great, but you don't want to be just a nice looking empty vessel; you want to have a positive spirit and a great attitude to fill your look.

It is very difficult to get other people, especially strangers, (especially interviewers) to believe things that you do not believe yourself. You need to think about the job you are applying for and "believe", "know" that you can do it. This does not mean that you already have to know how to do the job or that you have experience, it simply means that you have to believe that you can do whatever is required to do the job. If you have never done the type of work before or if you have never had a job before, you still must do some homework to understand what the job is about, determine to yourself if it is something you can and want to do. If it is, then you must have a positive attitude about it and express confidence that whatever is required, you can do.

Doubt and hesitation can kill you. If you act unsure or indecisive you will create doubts that you can, or even want, to do the job. When the interviewer asks you if you know what the job involves, at the very least you should have a basic idea and you should tell them. When they ask you if you can do the job, don't hmm and ha, don't say maybe, don't show doubt, don't hesitate; say "Yes". If you have doubts you need to keep them to yourself. It may help to know that everyone has doubts, but confident people keep their doubts to themselves.

Having confidence is not an accident, it is something you can work at. The type of person you appear to be is something you can work at. You can and must practice interviewing. When you walk into an interview everything should not be a surprise to you. You should have done it in your head many times before the actual interview itself. You should know the questions and the answers you will give. Your answers and questions should be prepared and rehearsed. You should have a mental list of the things that you want the interviewer to know about you and to remember about you. Many of the questions interviewers will ask and the types of answer you should give are covered here, but each individual is unique and you have to have your own answers in your own words readily at hand. Remember, being prepared will give you confidence.

Little things make a big difference

Little things combine to give you an aura of confidence and capability. Speaking clearly and at an easily audible level is very important. Speak as clearly as you can and speak so that the person sitting across from you can hear you without having to try. Remember it is much easier to speak up and speak clearly if you know what you are going to say.
Make eye contact. Look the person you are speaking to in the eye. Don't look away or at your feet. Don't look just in front of them or just beyond them, look at them.

Sit up straight in your chair. Don't slouch, don't hunch over, sit comfortable with your back straight. Try not to cross your legs or your feet. You won't be in the interview forever so this should not be that hard to do. All you have to do is be conscious of what you are doing at all times. Listen to yourself as you speak. Make a note to yourself that you are making eye contact. Make a note to yourself that you are sitting straight and that your legs and feet are not crossed. Chances are no one will do this perfectly and no one is suggesting that you be perfect, but if you "try" to be as perfect in these things as you can, you will be doing the best that you can and that is always acceptable.

If you are like most people you will experience nervousness before an interview. You will wonder if you will remember to do all of the things you would like to do while interviewing. Don't worry about it at that point. At that point you are there and you have prepared to the best of your ability. Most important, you are conscious and aware of what you have to and want to do. What is about to happen is not a mystery to you, it's something you have done before in your head. At that moment when you feel your nervousness coming on just relax. Close your eyes for a moment and take a deep breath. As your deep breaths are expelled your nervousness will leave with them. Try this at home before the interview along with everything else and you will see that it works.

The basic goal is to find confidence in yourself and share that confidence with others. Trust me, confidence is contagious; if you feel it, the person you are with will feel it too.

Some specifics

There are certain questions that you will be asked at every interview and as stated before, knowing the questions will help you to know and practice the answers. Here is a short list of questions and guidelines for constructing answers:

1. **Why do you want to work at X company?** Wal-Mart, the Imperial Palace, Target, Big O tires etc. - why do you want to work there? For the purpose of this section let's say the company in question is Wal-Mart. You want to work there because it's a big company, because they have good benefits, because the people there are nice, you shop there, your mother shops there, the store is clean, the store is bright, it has great prices, you will have a chance at a real career, you can grow with the company, you can learn lots of things, etc. etc. From a general point of view always remember this, if you go blank and can't think of a thing, just remember to "flatter" them, say something nice about the company, anything will do. If you totally blank out say something nice about the interviewer. Flattery always works.

2. **Why should they hire you.** In general the principle in the above example applies here, only now flatter yourself (within reasonable limits of course). I'm a hard worker, I work well with others, I'm always on time, I'm a fast learner, I'll do a great job for you, etc. However the two most important things are that you will always be on time and that you will never miss a shift. These are the two things that will definitely cost you a

job or lose you a job if you have one. Don't make it sound as if you will have any problems getting to work on time. In fact tell them that you believe it's better to be an hour early than a minute late. Another general rule is "no negative responses". Don't bring up any problems you may or may not have regarding any aspect of the job, period.

3. **Tell us what you liked about your last job.** I enjoyed working with the people, I enjoyed the work, I liked doing a good job.

4. **Tell us something you did not like about your last job.** NOTHING! Remember, no negative responses. Whatever the truth may or may not have been your response is that the job was just fine, you only left for whatever reason you listed on your application.

5. **What kind of people do you like to work with?** The answer is any type, you get along well with everyone.

6. **What kind of people don't you like to work with?** You can work with every type of person, you have never had a problem in this regard.

7. **What would you change about the policies and procedures of your last job if you could?** NOTHING! Again no negative responses. If you thought that your last employer was the worst company you could ever imagine and that a band of monkeys could do a better job than they were doing, keep it to yourself. No negative responses!

8. **If we called your last job what would they say about you?** They would say that I'm a hard worker, that I was always on time and that I got along with everyone, etc.

9. **Tell us something that you were criticized about at your last job.** Nothing!

10. **At your last job, if you saw someone doing something that they should not be doing (stealing for example) what would you do?** I would report it to my supervisor.

The ten questions above are questions you will almost certainly be asked at any interview in Las Vegas. Of course there are other questions but they are almost all variations of these. Just remember to listen to the question and answer the question you are being asked. Another important thing to remember is "No stories", just straight simple answers to the specific question asked to you. Don't give details that were not asked for, don't give details that have nothing to do with the question, don't tell stories about things that happened to you on or off the job. Just make eye contact, speak clearly and audibly and give them a clear simple answer.

Chapter Four

Jobs at Hotel Casinos

The good thing about hotel casinos is that they are always hiring.

They are open 24 hours a day and therefore must maintain a staff for all three shifts, day, swing and night (graveyard). The graveyard shifts are the most undesirable and therefore they are usually the ones that are most available.

Each hotel casino has its own way of hiring, its own policies and procedures. Most are what I call "long hires" meaning they take a long time to hire for their positions. But of course, not all of them are, just most. This is so for many reasons, some of the major ones are that they have a lot of personnel, which they can move around within their present employee population at any given moment. There are always people willing to work extra shifts if need be. They can demand that you work whatever shift they want whenever they want. Last of all, good planning, which allows them to fill their employment needs with the long view, meaning that they do not get caught short handed.

As I said, they are all different in their hiring practices and some are better than others. As an example the Station Casinos are a particularly long hire as a rule. They tell you that they will keep your application for six months and that they will call you within six months. Typically if you do not get hired you simply never hear from them again. The Imperial Palace on the other hand is just the opposite. When you apply there, typically, you will be interviewed the same day and often, if you seem suitable, you will be hired the same day. If you are not hired you will receive a post card within a week or two telling you that you did not get the position. I must point out to you that this is very unusual behavior in the Las Vegas employer community and you should not expect it. Las Vegas is a city where you can send out 50 resumes and not receive one response that your information has even been received.

Another example of different hiring practices is that the Station Casinos are, or at least seem to be, quite indifferent to the needs of the community. As an example, they don't appear to make any efforts to accommodate the disabled population. Again the Imperial Palace is just the opposite. They participate with numerous city and state agencies to accommodate the community and the disabled find employment with them. Of course, between these two extremes, expect everything and anything.

All hotel casinos share certain employment policies. All will subject you to a drug test and to a corporate background check. After you are hired, you will be sent for a drug test and a background check will be run on you. Take this very seriously. If you fail either, typically you cannot even apply for employment with them again for anywhere from six months to one year. Also it is not very likely that you will fail one casino's background check and pass another's. Because of this you must be completely prepared when you go to submit your application.

The drug test

The drug test is easy to prepare for, just don't do drugs. You must also remember that alcohol is considered a drug and is tested for. So do not drink before you go for your application. Remember, at a casino like the Imperial Palace, you could be hired the day you go to fill out your application. If you are, you will be sent immediately for a drug test. If you do not take the test within 24 hours (or less, it's up to the casino) you automatically fail. So the moral is, stop drinking well before you start submitting applications. As for drugs, for better or worse, the truth is that many people engage in what they consider to be harmless recreational drugs, like pot. Unfortunately pot takes quite a long time to leave your system. Most casinos only do a urine test, so a few weeks without either using pot or being around second hand smoke will usually do the trick. But if you have any question, whatsoever, in your mind about your ability to pass a drug test, do not go to do an application.

If you are not sure, there are basically two things you can do. One is to take a drug test yourself to see if you pass. This will cost you a few dollars but you will start your application process with a clear mind. The other thing you can do is avail yourself of many of the system cleaning products that are freely available all over the city. Just go to any Diversity store or to a GNC store and tell them what you need. Again, it will cost you a little money but it may save your job.

The corporate background check

If you fail the drug test, you're done. But if you fail the corporate background test you are just as done. Remember you must pass both the drug test and the corporate background test to be eligible to work for a hotel casino. The most painful part of failing either or both of these is that normally the casino only goes to the expense of ordering them "after" they have hired you. So failing them really means that after all you have gone through, you had the job and then lost it. You only get to take the corporate security check once, so you need to have it right the first time.

What the corporate security check does is check your background for lies, untruths or half-truths (there can be a difference). Mainly they look at your employment history and your criminal history.

Your employment history

All of the employment background checks are for the past 10 years. They want to know every job you have ever had in the past 10 years. By this they mean every job you have received a paycheck for, from a legitimate company (meaning they have filed a tax return on you). If you worked a job for one day and you were paid for that one day, they expect it to be listed on your application. If it is not listed on your application you fail the check and lose the job. You have lost the job in this case merely on a procedural formality. No one is suggesting that you intentionally lied about this or that you were trying to hide it. Their procedure simply automatically eliminates you for not having told them about it.

You must always include your dates of employment by month and year. You cannot simply say you worked from 1989 to 1999. You must give the month and the year and the dates must be accurate. Your job title and description must also be true. If you tell them you were in the accounting department and you really worked in the warehouse, you will fail. You must tell them what your beginning and ending salary was and this information must be accurate as well. Don't guess or just make this up. They will check this. You must provide an accurate address and phone number. If the phone number you give them for your former employer is wrong, they will not look it up for you and you will not pass. They will ask you for the name of your former supervisor, of course be as accurate as possible, but depending on how long ago the job was, you can be a tiny bit creative here. If the job was one year ago, it had better be the right name. If it was nine years ago any name will do in general because so much time has passed. So don't panic and not submit your application because you can't remember the full name of your supervisor from the job you worked for two months nine years ago. Also, though a full name is better, just a first name will do. Remember, they will call your past employers and ask them if you worked there, what dates you worked there, what your salary was, what your position was. For some of us it is fortunate that according to law they cannot ask your history at the company. Meaning they cannot ask if you were a real jerk or if you got fired for stealing all the inventory or running off with the boss's underage daughter. All they can ask is if they would hire you again. Of course the people who are calling about you and the people who are providing the information about you are counterparts in their various companies, so personal asides or heavy tonal inflections are always a possibility if your former employer really has it in for you, but there is nothing you can do about that, so don't worry about it.

Take note that it does not matter how far away your last job was, they will call to find out about your employment. OK, this really refers to the continental USA and Canada. If you have been here for two years and your jobs for the eight years prior to your arrival were all in your homeland in the Belgian Congo or mainland China, they are not going to call and in an instance like this it will be entirely up to them to decide how to handle it. It could go either way.

You must include three references who are not either former employers or relatives. These must be people whom they will have no trouble getting in touch with. The phone number you give for them must be correct and they must be readily available at this number to speak with them. They will call once or twice and they will leave a message (so make sure the person has voice mail) but that's it. You could run through everything with flying colors but have your entire application stalled because your references are not available.

Assuming all of your information is correct, they will then perform a quick analysis of your employment history. There are two major areas of concern here. One, any gaps in employment must be reasonably explained. The larger the gap the better your explanation must be. If you did not work for six months in 1999 they will ask you why and you need to know what you are going to tell them. If you did not work for three years between 1997 and 2000 they will really want to know why. Don't wing it, know what you are going to say and make sure it makes sense and is not illegal. Acceptable reasons might be you suffered an injury or you had to care for a relative, or you went back to school or were living on social security while deciding what you wanted to do. A not so acceptable reason might be that no one would hire you during this period of time or living on the streets, hustling, etc.

The second thing they will look at is why you left each job. When you moved from job A to job B, why? If you quit they will want to know if you gave job A proper notice that you were leaving to go to job B. Remember that whatever you did to your former employers they figure you will do to them. So whatever the case you must always have given your former employers formal and proper notice.

If you were fired/terminated from job A, you should be prepared to tell them why because they will ask. This can be a tricky point because there is usually no good reason to have been fired. But some are better than others and some reasons truly are not the fault of anything you did. Your challenge here will be to explain why you got fired in as positive a fashion as possible. A word of warning here, remember "Never" to give any negative responses, meaning don't say you were terminated because your supervisor hated you and had it in for you or because everyone had it in for you (at all cost avoid whining and blaming everything on "them"). Try saying that you had a misunderstanding with your supervisor. If you are asked what the misunderstanding was about you might say that it was of a personal nature and had little to do with the job. If you must tell them that you were fired, the idea is to minimize this fact as much as possible.

Most other reasons of why you left job A explain themselves; i.e., you were laid off, medical reasons, family reasons, etc. Again don't tell them anything that is not true. The fact that you were fired in and of itself, may not cost you the job, but the fact that you were dishonest about it definitely will.

They will also look at your job stability. If you have worked four different jobs in the last year and you only worked each job for a few weeks or months, it indicates that you are not stable and probably not reliable. If this is the case for you, again remember to try and have a reasonable explanation for it. An example of a reasonable explanation would be that you were in school during that year and tried to work when you could but needed to take time to study when necessary. If you have a background like this they may not ask you about it because they have dismissed you out of hand, so take the opportunity to explain it to them even if they don't ask.

If you have all of this under control you are ready to submit your application. The ideal situation would be that you have worked at one job for the last 10 years, you are leaving for a good reason and all is good in the world.

However this is almost never the case; in today's world, the era of the gold watch has long passed. Almost everybody has had at least a couple of jobs in the past 10 years and most people who are applying on the basic hotel casino job level have had many jobs. If you are a person who has kept good records and knows the address and phone number for every job you have had in the past 10 years, good for you. If you are the average person who may have had many jobs in the past 10 years of all sorts - temp positions, short term jobs, jobs for a year or two here or there, etc. - remembering your employment history accurately may not be so easy. It is very easy and very reasonable to forget a temp job you had eight years ago for two days. It's not intentional and you are not trying to hide anything, you are being as honest as you can be but you are only human. Still, not including that two-day job will cost you the job you just worked so hard to get.

Well, be of good cheer, because there is a simple solution to this. Go to the social security office and get a 10-year work history printout. This print out will include every job for which you have been legitimately paid and is the same information the casino will get when they run your background check, so you will be right on the money. When you go to the social security office and get in line you ask for it at the information window and they process it there, so you don't have to get a number and wait again. Now here is where you make money by reading this. The printout costs $35 dollars and at $35 dollars it's cheap considering the security it will give you. But when you request it if you tell them it is for "metro" (meaning the police) they will give it to you for "free" - so I have just given you $35 in cash.

Unfortunately now that you have your printout there is more work for you to do. The printouts are hard to read. At first sight they don't appear to make any sense at all and you can't just hand them the printout, you still have to fill out the application and the printout does not actually contain all of the information you will need on the application.

The printout will list all of the jobs you have had by year. Go to a line that says total income for X year and read up from there to the next line that says the same thing but for a different year. All of the jobs above total income for 1994 will be all of the jobs you had that year. It will include the name and address of the company, but NOT THE PHONE NUMBER. You now know the year you worked there but NOT THE MONTH YOU STARTED OR THE MONTH YOU ENDED. If you worked for a company for many years you will have to go back to the first year you see the company listed and up to the last year you see it listed to know which years you were there. If you have overlapping employment, you will have to explain this, (i.e., full time and one part-time job), but you still will not have your starting and ending months. If you worked for a company with many locations, the address they give and the name of the company will probably be the corporate head quarters. So you have a little work cut out for you. You must look up the phone number for each company. You must call them to get your start and end dates. You must know, or find out if you don't know, for example that Green Star Corp. at 11111 Oak Dr., NYC, is the corporate headquarters for the local Wendy's you worked for in Florida and call them to get the local address of the store where you actually worked. You must then put all of this information in order from the current date running back 10 years. Don't wait until you go to do your application to do this. Have it all figured out and neatly written down so when you go to do your application all you have to do is copy it. If you do, this you will not have a problem.

Chapter Five

The retail employment community

Next to the hotel and casino community, the Las Vegas retail community is perhaps the second largest employer, and of this group Wal-Mart is clearly number one. For this reason I will devote this section to finding employment at Wal-Mart. **The things you will discover here will assist you in finding employment with any retail company, large or small, not just Wal-Mart.**

There is an age-old saying which states, "forewarned is forearmed", meaning that if you know what is going to happen, you are better prepared for it. Preparation is a continuing theme in this book. In every section there is talk about knowing what is going to happen and preparing for it by practicing what you will do and say when the moment comes.

Wal-Mart

Why Wal-Mart?

Why have I chosen Wal-Mart as the example to use and why should you think of Wal-Mart as a possibility?

Wal-Mart is the biggest retail company, not just in the world, but also in the history of the world, with total annual sales exceeding 200 billion dollars. It is also interesting to note that this enormous amount is also three or four times more than the annual sales of the No. 2 retail company.

So when you consider Wal-Mart, you are considering a major corporate opportunity that is available to you. In other words, you can grow both with and in Wal-Mart. You can start out pushing carts in the parking lot and end up as a super center manager. So if you like, or grow to like, the retail industry, working for Wal-Mart provides you with both a major retail education (which you can use at any retail company) and an opportunity to be a part of the major company of its type on the planet and to grow to be all that you can be within the company.

Wal-Mart is so big that they are always looking for people to promote into more responsible positions. Like the hotel and casino industry, they are also so big that they are constantly hiring. As you need more and more employees, your turnover of employees increases proportionately. So on any given day in Las Vegas one of the six Wal-Mart super centers or one of the five Wal-Mart Stores is hiring (not to even mention their Sam's Club operation). In a city and a world, where so many jobs are flat out dead-end, Wal-Mart provides an opportunity for the average person to be part of an ever-growing team and make a difference for themselves and their family.

Another benefit of Wal-Mart is that they are both national and international. This means that as a member of the Wal-Mart family you have the opportunity to transfer from state to state or even to another country, if there is an opening for you. It may take time but they are very accommodating in this way to good employees and will do all they can to help you.

Wal-Mart also provides one of the best benefits programs in Las Vegas. So much so that there are people who maintain a full time job there just so their family can take advantage of the benefits. In addition to great medical and dental benefits they have both a 401-K retirement plan and a stock-option plan. There are long time Wal-Mart employees who over the years have become relatively rich through their Wal-Mart stock.

Because Wal-Mart is a 24-hour operation, every conceivable shift is possible. As you work and prove yourself, they will accommodate you in helping you have a shift that works better for you. Of course, as I just said, you have to earn this, but the important thing is that it is possible. So if you are uncertain about what you want to do or if you are looking for a new career, Wal-Mart is certainly something to consider. However, Wal-Mart also works for the many people who just need a job to get by at the moment. It might be a good way to keep yourself alive until you find and get the job you are really looking for.

Here is a detailed description of the Wal-Mart hiring process, which will be instructive for any company where you plan to apply here in

Las Vegas. A suggestion about Wal-Mart employment opportunities: apply at the super centers, rather than the regular Wal-Mart stores. The super centers are many times bigger (each store is 225,000 sq ft) and each store employs upwards of 700 people, so they are very active in the hiring arena. If possible you should apply at a store that is, relatively speaking, the least accessible. As an example the super center at 4505 W. Charleston is right in the middle of town, near many residential areas, bus lines, etc. and is very easy to get to by the local population. For this reason there is a great pool of local people for the store to draw upon for employees, which for you means that their need for employees is easily fed. The super center at 8060 Tropical Parkway, located at the Centennial Parkway exit, north of Ann Road on I95, is in a more upscale residential area (meaning that the more affluent population of the area is not as prone to want to work there) and no matter how close you live to it, it is only convenient to get there by car. Public transportation is available but not easy. For these reasons they have to look harder for employees. They don't have a problem with employees who have to travel 2 hours or more to work each day by bus, because they need people and the people who want to work there often come from neighborhoods that are that far away. The West Charleston store has many more applicants and options and as a result, they are a slow hire, meaning they take their sweet time. The Tropical Parkway store is as busy a store but has fewer applicants, so in general they tend to be a fast-hire location, meaning when they need people they need them now and they hire quickly to meet their needs. I might point out that this concept works equally well regarding any retail store, Albertson's, Smith's, Vons's, Target, etc.

The Wal-Mart application can be picked up at the lay-away counter located at the back of any store. Just go there and ask for one. The application is a short one but, unless you have read this book, I would suggest you take it with you and fill it out at home.

One of the things Wal-Mart has in common with the hotel and casino industry is an insistence on open availability. Wal-Mart will only consider you for employment if you are available to work at anytime, whenever they need you and can schedule you. This is not surprising; remember that employers hire you for their convenience not yours. There is a section that asks when you are available to work, on which days and from what hours to what hours. They tend to like military time in this answer, so put that you are available from 00:00 to 24:00 every day, seven days a week. You can work holidays, weekends, whenever, and you want whatever is available, day, swing, or night shifts. This does not mean that you will actually get a shift you don't prefer; it just means that you will accept any shift. If they have many positions open, during the interview they may even ask what shift you would prefer and let you choose from those available. Remember, if you don't do this you will NOT get a job. Where it asks you what position you are applying for put at least two choices one of which should be "any". This way if they do not have your first choice available you can ask what they do have available.

If you have applied at other Wal-Mart stores it is not necessary to mention it unless you are asked directly. Remember each store is an autonomous operation, so if one store does not hire you it is fine to apply at another one.

Be as detailed as possible with your work history, they will call to verify your past employment. See the section called the "interview" for detail on how to complete this section of the application.

One of the most important sections of their application is the personal references request. This may seem like a simple, easy and basically unimportant thing, but it is key to processing your application. They will not schedule you for an interview if they cannot get at least two references for you. This means that the people you give them as references must be reachable, preferably during business hours. There have been so many times when really great candidates have been sent home to come in another day because they could not contact their references. So don't take this lightly, make sure that whomever you chose to put down is reachable, preferably beginning with the day you turn in your application.

Depending upon the activity at the store and the needs of the store on the day you submit your application, you will either be asked to wait until you are called to come in for an interview or if you are lucky, you may be interviewed that day.

You will have 4 interviews, an eligibility interview by someone from the personnel office, two interviews by assistant managers and a final interview by the store manager or co-manager. Each interviewer will ask you more or less the same questions put in different ways. Remember the basic questions and remember the basic approach to answering all questions. There is information pertaining to this in the section entitled "the interview" Below is a list of questions specifically related to the retail employment community, read it carefully.

Why do you want to work for Wal-Mart (why Wal-Mart?)

Why should Wal-Mart hire you?

These are always the two leading questions. Always remember the basic approach to answering all questions of this type, i.e., flattery. So your answers would be something like:

1. **Why Wal-Mart?** – You want to work for Wal-Mart because they are a large company, because they are the best at what they do, because the store is clean, because the people who work there are friendly, because your family shops there, because they can offer you a chance to grow and have a career, etc.
2. **Why should Wal-Mart hire you?** – Because you are a hard worker, because you are always on time, because you always do the best you can, because you are a fast learner, because you have always wanted to work for a company like them, etc.

There will also be questions about your past employment or school history and what the people there thought of you. For example:

Tell us something about your last job that you were proud of.
Tell us something about your last job that you were praised for.
Tell us something about your last job that you did not like.
Tell us what you did not like about your last supervisor.
Tell us about a problem you had with a supervisor at your last job and what you did about it.
Tell us about a problem you had with a customer and what you did about it.
Tell us something that your supervisor criticized you for.
What would you change about the way your last employer did business?
What rules and regulations would you change at your last job?
What kind of people do you like to work with?
What kind of people don't you like to work with?
What do you look for in a supervisor?
What do you think makes a good supervisor?
If you saw someone doing something wrong (stealing, drinking, etc.) on the job, what would you do about it?

The basic rule to follow when answering all of these questions is **"NO NEGATIVE RESPONSES"**. Here are some examples.

1. How did they feel about you – everyone liked me.
2. Something you were proud of – always being on time and doing my best.
3. Something you were praised for – always paying attention to the job.
4. Something you did not like – nothing.
5. What you did not like about your supervisor – nothing.
6. A problem you had with your supervisor – none.
7. A problem you had with a customer – none.
8. Something you were criticized for – nothing.
9. What would you change – nothing.
10. What rules would you change – none.
11. What kind of people do you like to work with – all types.
12. What kind of people don't you like to work with – I like all people.
13. What you look for is a supervisor that will give you a chance to learn the job.
14. What makes a good supervisor – one who listens and is fair.
15. What would you do if you saw someone doing something wrong? – Report it to the supervisor.

Remember **NO NEGATIVE RESPONSES!**

The second basic rule to answering all questions is **"NO STORIES"**.

For example, "tell me what kind of people you like to work with".

"Well I like to work with people who are nice, I like to work with all types of people, and I have no problem getting along with anyone. It's like my aunt Molly once told me when I was visiting her in Georgia. She was sitting outside on the swing and her two boys had just run off to help uncle Oscar pick cotton. She was just sitting there and shucking corn and smiling like she always does, when she looked up and said to me. You know, she said, when the boys was little I always told them…"

Stop at "Well I like to work with people who are nice, I like to work with all types of people, and I have no problem getting along with anyone"; just answer the question. I like to work with all types of people is really enough. **NO STORIES!** Even if they are great stories nobody has time for them and in general the more you say the worse it is for you. Be sure to listen to the question and answer it as simply and clearly as possible. And make sure you answer the question they asked you.

They will also give you an opinion survey. Remember in general to answer the questions the way a sweet innocent person would. Even if you don't think there is a difference between alcohol and pot, remember the law does and so does the store. The answers to the questions are not about what you think; they are about what they want to hear.

The Orion opinion survey is four pages of just under 70 questions designed to evaluate the applicant's mental, psychological and spiritual inclinations toward honesty, drug and alcohol abuse and other traits not good for the company.

Many of the questions are tricky and many of them are obscure with no clear point of view. These questions are answered on a scale of 1 to 10, 1 being you "totally disagree" and 10 being you "totally agree". Remember to only answer "1" totally disagree or "10" totally agree and none of the options in between.

Here are some examples of the questions and the proper answers.

1. "I used to use drugs before going to work but I don't do that any more". –
   This is one of many two-part questions. I "used to" but I "don't now". You must answer the first part of these questions not the second. In this case the answer is that you "completely disagree" because you never used drugs. Don't respond to the second part, which is that you don't do this now. It's true that you don't do it now, but it's truer that you never did it.

2. "Frank and Pete go to lunch and drink and smoke pot, but it does not affect their ability to do a good job when they return to work. What they did was OK". - Here you "completely disagree" again because corporate culture dictates that it is not the effect of drug use but the fact of drug use that is unacceptable.

3. "Bill was a good manager and had over 100 people under him. One day his boss tells him to fire Joe because Joe is not doing a good job. Bill knows that Joe is having problems at home so rather than firing Joe he puts him in a position where his boss

will not see him. Sure enough, two weeks later Joe's problems at home are gone and he is doing a really great job. Bill did the right thing under the circumstances". – Again you "totally disagree" because although Bill's opinion of the situation was correct, he disobeyed a direct order by his superior, which is a no-no.

4. "Harry spent two hours balancing his checkbook only to find that he was 15 cents off at the end. He then spent four hours finding out where he made the 15-cents mistake. Harry wasted his time doing this". – You "totally disagree" because no price is too high for doing things the right way.

5. "If someone is caught stealing, under some circumstances, they should be given a second chance. Again, you totally disagree because a thief is a thief and stealing is totally unacceptable.

6. A person who is steals is almost never caught". – You "totally disagree" because the company view is that a person who steals is always caught no matter what.

7. "Someone who is caught stealing should be exposed publicly". This is one of the either/or questions. If you say yes (you totally agree) they will ask you why and the answer is that public exposure will discourage others from stealing. If you say no, (you totally disagree) they will ask why and the answer is that public exposure will let other people know that the system can be robbed, which they discourage. So answer either way, just know why.

8. "I used to come into work late but I know better now and I don't do it any more". – Again this is one of the two part questions. Answer the first part. You "totally disagree" because you have never been late.

9. "An employee should defend his company when other people are criticizing it". – This is one of the "totally agree" questions because they want you to be a part of the team through and through.

10. "Most people succeed in business by hard work and dedica-
tion" – This is another "totally agree" question because this is
the American way

On the last page, at the very end, there are 10 or 12 questions all of
which are about work place safety. You "totally disagree" with all of
these. Read them or not, just remember to totally disagree with them.
Also remember to only answer "1", I totally disagree or "10", I totally agree. Don't use any of the options between two and nine. If you
use the underlying principles demonstrated by these examples you will
do just fine on the Orion or any opinion survey.
Also remember that just about every large retail organization has
some form of opinion survey of its own, asking questions which try and
discover the same things about you as Wal-Mart's "Orion" survey, so
the skills you learn from Orion will guide you wherever you apply.
The last person to interview you is the manager or co-manager of
the store. If you followed what is outlined here they should offer you a
job. Unfortunately if they do not offer you a job but tell you that they
will call you, you probably did not get the job.
If you get the job you will have to go for a drug test. If you fail the
drug test you will not get the job and you will not be able to apply
again for six months or a year. If you pass the drug test they will call
you and you will have to go into the store for your orientation. At this
point congratulations, you've got yourself a job.

News Flash!

The application system at Wal-Mart and most of the major retail chains
has recently changed from paper applications to computer applications.
All of the information contained in this chapter remains the same, only
the manner of submitting it has changed. Rather than asking for an application and filling it out either at the store or at home, you now have
to fill it out at one of several computer application terminals located in
the store. Normally they are either in the customer service area or the
lay-away area. They are either filled out using a computer keyboard or
a monitor touch screen. Normally you have to do some of both. If you
cannot type you can hunt and peck to input items like your name, address and employment history. If you have difficulty reading, inform a
store manager and they will assign someone to assist you. But in general you must be able to read and write. You must still prepare for the

application as instructed in this chapter. You should have all of your employment information with you and ready to be copied to the computer application. The opinion survey is now a part of the computer application so be prepared to take it when you apply. The entire process takes about an hour to complete, but the more organized and prepared you are the quicker you will finish.

Before you go to fill out the application it is a good idea to call the human resources department at the store you will apply at to find out what positions are available. This way you can apply for an opening that they are looking to fill immediately. After completing the application call the human resources department again and tell them that your application is now in the system. If you can call them before you leave the store, tell them you have just done it and have not left the store as yet. This way you may get lucky and get to either see someone right away or set up an appointment for an interview right away.

Chapter Six

Quick-hire / Slow-hire jobs

This is a convenient way to separate jobs that you are likely to get hired for soon or right away and jobs where you are not likely to get hired soon or right away.

Quick hire jobs

Jobs that do not require any specific experience would fit into the 'no resume required' category. These would be jobs either with a certain type of company or of a certain type or both. Examples of a certain type of company would be small companies with staffs of five to 10 and up. They don't have middle management and their needs are usually immediate.

Some large companies like certain hotel casinos or retail companies, which have a large turnover and are set up to constantly feed certain types of positions. The types of job available in either of these types of company are similar. Kitchen workers, housecleaners, housekeepers, lawn repair and maintenance workers, seasonal workers, cab and limo drivers, dishwashers, short-order cooks, stock people, cart pushers, clean- up workers, sales people, door-to-door people, appointment setters, telemarketers, survey takers, certain types of customer service workers, ride attendants, cashiers, and many variations on these general themes.

Indicators of a quick-hire business

1. They do not ask for a resume to be sent to them.
2. They have a phone number to call them directly.
3. They ask you to come in ASAP to fill out an application.

4. They ask you about your experience over the phone.
5. They need many people to fill the same position or positions.
6. They tell you about the job on the phone (hours, salary etc.).
7. They interview you when you turn in your application.
8. And, of course, when they hire you on the spot.

Slow-hire jobs

A slow-hire job is any one that requires extensive skills or experience and the accompanying resume, any job with a city, state or federal agency, program or facility. The jobs in the first category typically require an in-depth and therefore lengthy recruiting process to properly screen all eligible candidates and finally pick the "right one". Jobs in the second category, even if it is a simple cleaning or sorting job requiring no special skills, is subject to red tape and bureaucracy. Expect jobs in either of these categories to take many months to fill. In either case it could literally be months before they even acknowledge receipt of your resume.

Indicators of a slow-hire business

1. You can only mail in your resume.
2. You can fax in your resume but there is no contact phone number.
3. You are told they are accepting applications.
4. You are told they are always accepting applications.
5. You must make an appointment for an initial interview through an automated telephone voice system.
6. You are told to drop off your application and you will be contacted.
7. You are told they will keep your application of file for six months.
8. You can apply via the Internet.
9. You can find available jobs via the Internet.
10. You are told they are accepting applications until a date in the future.
11. Their advertisement only appears once (indicating that they must run a public advertisement due to some regulation but already know who they will hire).

Chapter Seven

Temporary Employment Agencies

There are several temporary agencies here in Las Vegas. Just pick up the phone book and try the one nearest to you. If you find yourself in a bind where you need fast cash there are temp agencies that hire out day labor. Generally they also pay daily. The work is generally physical labor of some sort. If you are lucky the job may last for more than one day, if you are both lucky and really good, the employer may offer you a job and keep you (don't look forward to this.). Labor Ready would be an example of this type of temporary agency.

If you have skills there are also any number of temp agencies that can get you temporary assignments. As an example if you are a bookkeeper or accountant, you can sign up with an agency like Robert Half/Acutemps, as they deal specifically with your industry. There are agencies like this for most professions; again the phone book will lead you where you need to go.

Just remember that this is just what it is advertised as being, "a temporary" solution to your employment problem.

Chapter Eight

Local, State and Federal Jobs

Local, State and Federal agencies and programs are, in general, always accepting applications. The emphasis here is on "accepting applications" as opposed to hiring.

These jobs usually have a set period for accepting applications. Sometimes this period can be for as much as a month or more, which means that if you apply at the beginning of the period, when the job is first listed, you will have to wait an entire month before your application is even reviewed.

Also these positions typically involve an examination of some kind, which means that you may have to wait X period of time until the exam is being given. Perhaps it is not typical, but I have seen it take an individual up to two years to successfully obtain a position of this type.

One can easily find out what positions are available and what the requirements are, either on the Internet or by stopping by a local "Nevada Job Links" office where you will find this information both posted and available by using their computer room, which is free and open to the public for job searches.

Chapter Nine

What if You Have a Disability?

T his section is for the many individuals who may be eligible for assistance but who are not aware of it.

There are many people that have disabilities, some minor and some severe. It is important both for the applicant and the employer to remember that disabilities are not necessarily debilitating. Sometimes they may require accommodations and sometimes not, but either way it is important not to let your disability interfere with your desire or ability to get a job if you want one.

There are agencies in the Las Vegas community whose sole purpose is to assist people with disabilities. In terms of employment, they not only help individuals find suitable employment but they assist them with the training and counseling necessary to have a job. Some agencies go so far as to assist you with schooling for employment, clothing, tools, gas for your car or a bus pass, even job coaching to help you learn the job if needed. They even teach people how to ride the bus.

Although many people take advantage of these programs, there are many people who are eligible for this assistance who do not realize it, don't know where to go for it, or are too proud to admit or accept that they have a definable disability. Many have a misunderstanding of what constitutes a disability or of the imagined stigmas that accompany them.

As I mentioned in the beginning of this section, a disability is not necessarily debilitating. There are conditions that fall within the range of legitimate disabilities that do not fit the common sense idea of what a disability is. Here are some examples of disability that I would place in this category. Any sort of accident which you may have had, that impairs your 100% performance, no matter how long ago you had it. So if you had a knee injury at work ten years ago and as a result you cannot stand or lift as long as might be expected you qualify as a person with a disability. If you have asthma or another condition which requires attention, that's a disability. You could be 100% physically and mentally fit, but if you are a convicted felon, the fact that you have been to jail is considered a disability. If you have trouble with reading, writing or math you have a disability. The point is that a disability need not be severe; in fact, it may not have inconvenienced you at this point in your life. Perhaps you have had jobs where college level reading or good math skills were not required, so you have never thought of yourself as having a disability. Of course people who have severe disabilities know it and live with it on a day-to-day basis and in all likelihood are and have been receiving assistance.

It is not necessary to make anything up; all I am suggesting is that you objectively think about yourself and consider if you may be eligible. If you think that you are, or might be, there is no shame in it but there are many useful benefits as stated above. From the employment viewpoint, one of the services individuals with disabilities have, that are not normally available to the general population, is job development.

The agencies that assist you, when they think you are prepared and ready, assign you a job developer. This is a highly trained professional whose sole task is to find you gainful employment. It is a unique and personal service. They work on a case-by-case basis to find employment to match the specific person. Their job is to find you a job that you can do and an employer who will give you the opportunity to do it.

For their clients with severe disabilities, for example, individuals who are wheelchair bound, they seek to find employers who will make accommodations for the wheelchair in their work place. For individuals with mild or relatively non-interfering conditions, such as asthma, they provide job counseling, assistance with identifying available work (who is hiring, for what and for how much at that moment); as well as assistance in the form of personal introductions to prospective employers and transportation to and from interviews when required.

These job developers are paid by the state or federal agency that you are dealing with, so there is no expense to you.

For more information about this call the Nevada Bureau of Vocational Rehabilitation at 702-486-5230, you can also write to them at 628 Belrose St., Las Vegas, NV 89107.

Chapter Ten

What it is Like to Find a Job in Las Vegas

I f you are one of the five to seven thousand people who move to Las Vegas each month, this book is a must read for you. If you are one of the vast number of unemployed or under-employed residents of Las Vegas, this book is also a must read for you. If you are one of the five to six thousand people who move out of Las Vegas each month, this book might have changed your future dramatically; and if you decide to try Las Vegas again, it will.

The purpose of this book is to give you an overview of the employment market here in Las Vegas and to provide you with the knowledge and tools necessary to find a job here.

There is a section about what makes Las Vegas a unique, job-seeking, environment. Because this work is meant to be a practical one, this section is found at the end. The beginning sections are devoted to the actual job market here. What types of jobs are available, how readily they are available and what to look for and expect as you engage in your job search. Other sections deal with how to prepare yourself for finding a job. The things you need to do and not do and what employers are looking for and how to give it to them. The final section is a workbook, which will help you get ready to hit the streets and get a job.

Las Vegas, a unique place

Las Vegas, Nevada, is as unique a place to live and work, as it is to visit and have fun. Most people around the world have one image of Las Vegas burned into their consciousness. A glitzy, fast paced town where one goes to have an experience of the fast life and a good time. Every movie you see of Las Vegas shows the glittering strip, afire with thousands of lights and thousands of people milling around smiling, gambling, drinking and having fun. When you think of Las Vegas, no matter where you may be from or what you look like or what background you come from, you think of beautiful women, handsome men and most of all, money.

Las Vegas is portrayed as a dream town, a Camelot where the poorest, dumbest slob can, with just a little luck, hit it rich. The casinos are open to everyone; anyone can play and anyone, including you, can win. The myth of Las Vegas is so strong that it is one of the only places in the world where people love to go and plan to lose money. Just imagine the 30 million visitors a year who come to Las Vegas, planning their trip and including in the trip budget an item of "how much we can afford to lose". Although everyone comes here with the dream, spoken or unspoken, of winning, 99% out of 100% come here with the sure, planned ahead knowledge, that they are going to lose, not win.

Of the 30 million people a year who visit here, there is a tiny percentage who consider moving here and an even a smaller percentage that actually do. Remember, the total population of Las Vegas is somewhere between 1 million and 1.5 million; this means that the total population is only 1.5% of the people who visit here each year, which also means that 98.5% of the people who are here every year are strangers. When you stop and think about it, you will realize that this has a dramatic effect on the lifestyle and employment environment of the people who chose to live here.

Las Vegas is also unique in that it is largely a one-industry town where gambling is king. This is a town, which was conceived of, and created to accommodate the gaming industry, and there are no industries, agencies, politicians, individuals, dogs or cats, who are not impacted upon or influenced by the gaming industry. Even if you have a job as far away from the gaming industry as possible, you are still affected by the gaming industry as every industry in Vegas services the hotels and casinos in someway. At first thought you might say that this isn't really true. How about apartment complexes - they don't have slot machines in them and the casinos do not own them. True, but the vast majority of the people who live in them work in the gaming industry and the housing here was created for gaming people or people in business who support gaming to live. This is true of supermarkets, department stores, government agencies, everyone.

Because three out of five people work for a hotel & casino, they get to do the picking and choosing. In the end, if you want to work for one of them, it's their way or the highway. This is a right-to-work state, and they can hire you and fire you as they wish, with no explanation. This is one of the reasons why it is so important to know what they require and how to give it to them in the proper way, which is what you will learn here.

Vegas is also unique in its topography. Las Vegas is an island, one not surrounded by water, but by sand. This geographical isolation has a profound effect on surviving and finding employment here. In just about every other part of the country, life and therefore job opportunities, exist in extended areas or communities. As an example, New York, New Jersey and Connecticut, are called the tri-state Area, meaning that they interact and can be interacted with on a daily basis for all of the necessities of life. Brooklyn, New York, which is just one of the five boroughs, has a population of over a million people, which makes it about as populous as Vegas. The employment possibilities in Brooklyn are many and varied. If you lived in Brooklyn and wanted to work in Brooklyn, no matter what field you were in, from common laborer to high priced attorney, you could find something to do there. But let's suppose that for some reason you had burned all of your bridges in Brooklyn. Would your working life be over? By no means, as you could then look for a job in Manhattan, or Queens or any of the five boroughs of New York city, and have as many or more options as you had staying in Brooklyn. The amazing thing is that each borough has a unique culture of its own and has employers who are in no way connected to the other boroughs. You are now in a community of eight million people and millions of job possibilities. To take it one last step, let's suppose that you don't want to or can't work in New York City; you can now reasonably explore New Jersey and Connecticut, and the reverse is even truer. You can live in Connecticut or New Jersey and commute to NY to work. The point is that you have to fail in an awful lot of places to fail to find a job in the tri-state area.

Not so in Vegas - As Vegas is land-locked, if you want to live here you have to make it in the Valley or leave. There is no alternative; it is find a job here or leave here, period. So once again, if you want to live here, whatever your reasons, you need to be as prepared as possible before you venture out into the job market. Perhaps you don't realize it but for most jobs in Vegas, if you are turned down or fail to pass part of the employment process, you cannot even apply again for six months to one year.

Our unique topographical situation has other impacts on living here. On a clear day if you look in any direction you will see mountains.

We literally live in a valley, in a bowl. The natural consequence of this is air inversion. This, combined with the dust of endless construction and ever growing amounts of automobile fumes, creates a health hazard.

If you drive to the far east or the far west some morning as the sun is rising and look back down at the strip, you will most likely see a dense brown cloud sitting on top of the city. That wet blanket sitting there, smothering the breathable air, is the result of air inversion. You can't see it when you are in the middle of it, but that brown soup is what you breathe all day when you are working or playing in town.

Add to this the near zero humidity and you have a serious health condition. The heat and low humidity dry out your mucus membranes, which is your first line of defense against air-born irritants and the infections which can result from them. Las Vegas is a very sickly place. Many first-time inhabitants suffer from nosebleeds for up to a year as their mucus membranes vanish. Everyone here is subject to colds, flu and sinus infection continuously throughout the year.

Living in the cold northeast, I almost never had a cold or flu, but here they are yearly friends. Vegas is the only place I know that has epidemics of biblical proportions. During the winter of '96 or '97, there was an upper-respiratory infection that overran the valley to the extent that valley hospitals announced on the radio and TV not to come to the hospital because there was no room and there was nothing they could do for you. The pharmacies ran out of medication.

More recently the same thing happened again in the winter of 2003. It is unnerving to hear health officials announce all week on radio and television that they are down to 300 doses of flu vaccine in a town of 1.5 million people, especially at a time when the entire country is being hit, by an influenza type flu and children are dying from it.

Add to this, 30 million strangers from all over the face of the earth, and you find yourself in a living germ pool of global proportions. How can this not affect employment here?

Our geographical location also adds hard twists to basics, like water and sewer, rendering Vegas very much like a third world nation, where you can't drink the water or breathe the air. The tap water in Vegas is not drinkable, creating yet another health hazard.

One of the geographical characteristics of Vegas, which is easy to miss on the face of it, is that it is such a small town. The media image of Vegas leads one to the illusion that it is a large sprawling metropolis, filled with millions of glittering lights, which stretches out endlessly to the horizon in every direction. The truth, as all who live here know, is that all of those wonderful shots are of one street and one street only. Once you leave the strip you tumble into Small Townsville. Suddenly the 24-hour fun/adventure town becomes a sleepy bedroom community where the local bars are deserted by 10 p.m. and closed by midnight. By 11 p.m. you can't find a place to eat outside of a casino.

The glamour of millions of dollars, fancy people and fabulous salaries vanishes into cheap villas. In a place where Zigfried and Roy make 53 million dollars a year, plus, and Danny Gans (whom no one has ever heard of outside of the business in Vegas) gets paid $500,000 a week, the average working person is suddenly confronted with a city that hates to pay him even $10 an hour. The hotel casinos make fabulous amounts of money and they pay fabulous salaries to the top chosen few, but beyond that, it's a slave city. It is estimated that there are, more or less, three employees for every hotel room; so in a hotel such as the Bellagio, with approximately 3600 rooms, that would mean more or less 10,800 employees. The average wage for 98% of those employees is probably less than $10 an hour. The Vegas the movies portray and that the tourists come to visit is not the Vegas that 98% of the people who live here live in.

The truth is that Vegas is a very small, provincial, cowboy town. If you consider that 10 years ago the population here was around 500,000 it means that the other million people who are now here are outsiders. Of course, the people who have been here for 30+ years have made lots of money and, even more important, they all know each other. Vegas is a prototypical "good old boy" town and not just in the gambling community, but in every business that exist, both private and public. Vegas is a town where it is much better to have the right friends than the right credentials or abilities. It is important to remember this, not just when you are looking for a job, but also when you have one and are looking to advance. This is not a performance town, doing the best job will not get you the best results.

Politics is, of course, controlled by money, which means the town is controlled by gambling interest. How else could a town so rich have to raise taxes on the poor to pay for the worst education system and the worst social service system in the country? Teachers flee Vegas every year by the thousands because teaching jobs, even in the backwoods of just about anyplace else in America, pay more and have far superior benefits than Vegas does. Homeless shelters here are not only filled, but also closing for lack of money to support them. Las Vegas has a high (if not the highest) high school dropout rate in the country, and one of the lowest college admissions and graduation rates. Just about everybody here who can come up with two cents to rub together sends their kids to a private school.

Vegas, for the most part, is not a nice or a friendly place to be an employee. It is a right-to-work state, which could rephrase to mean that it is a right-to-fire, without a cause, reason or explanation, state. Of course you have the right to quit without reason or explanation also, but where don't you have that right. Of course, if you, as an employee, actually do that here, you will be digging your own grave because quitting without notice is a grave offense in the hotel casino world.

Our Office of Employment Discrimination is famous for doing nothing.

Vegas is now also a union town. In 1996 the AFL/CIO launched a major attack to unionize Las Vegas, the result of which is that now all but one or two hotel casinos are unionized.

All in all, it is simply good to remember that whatever your experiences in the job market were in other places, it will have little to do with your experiences here. If I sent out 50 resumes in New York City, I would get 50 replies, at the very least acknowledging that my resume had been received. I can tell you from actual experience that sending out 50 resumes in Las Vegas typically results in a loud silence, meaning zero responses. Sending out resumes in Las Vegas is almost a nonevent.

So be prepared for many obstacles when looking for a job (be prepared for many obstacles after you find one too). Contrary to the media image of Vegas as a land of golden opportunity, finding a job here is tough and finding a meaningful job here is a serious challenge. But there are jobs here, and my job is to help you get what's available by preparing for the realities of the Las Vegas job experience.

Conclusion

As of December 2003, the entire country, due to our military activities in Iraq, has been in a form of upheaval, which unfortunately has a negative effect on the employment market. This effect is magnified many times here in Las Vegas where we are now a state that had to go to its supreme court to get an unconstitutional budget which resulted in a billion dollar tax increase. The immediate effect of this has been waves of layoffs in the public sector and among the vendors that serve the public sector. Enormous resources devoted to protection from terrorism or consumed by historical business scandals, such as Enron and World-Com; wars, excessive political abuses and greed have all combined to create an unfriendly atmosphere for the average guy simply looking to support his family.

Now is not the best time to be in the job market, as I am sure you have discovered for yourself. The jobs, on every level from high to low which are available, will experience new highs in competition as more and more people compete for fewer jobs and as more qualified workers compete for low skill work.

The good news is that if you read this book carefully and follow its prescriptions, you will have a much better than even chance of getting a job. In fact I can all but guarantee that you will get a job. I am not saying that you will get the job of your dreams; what I am saying is that you will have work, a means of support to carry on with your life while you continue to prepare yourself and look for your dream job.

Happy Job Hunting and GOOD LUCK!

Workbook

T he purpose of this workbook is to help you organize all of the information you will need for your job search. If you complete this workbook you should have no problem filling out any application for a job.

In the Employment History section, remember you need a "ten year" employment history, so add as many pages as you may need to this section to make it complete.

 Good luck!!!

Personal history

Name:

Present address:

Number of years at present address:

Previous address:

Number of years at previous address:

Current telephone number:

Social security number:

Talents and Hobbies:

Church:

Organization memberships:

Emergency contact person, name, address, phone number and relationship:

Personal references: (not related to you) name, address and phone number

1.

2.

3.

Educational History

High School attended:

Address:

Years completed:

Attended, from: To:

Graduated: Yes____   No _____

Diploma: Yes _____   No_____

Sports:

Clubs:

Awards:

Area of study:

College:

Address:

Years completed:
Attended, from: to:

Graduated: Yes_____   No _____

Degree: Yes _____   No_____

Degree in:

Sports:

Clubs:

Awards:

Special interest:

Additional education or training:

Employment history

#1

Last Job

Name of employer:

Address:

Reachable phone number:

Name of supervisor:

Your Job title:

Your job description:

Dates of employment: from_____ to_____
(Mo., day, year)

Special recognition at job:

Reason you are no longer at this job:

#2

Job Before Last

Name of employer:

Address:

Reachable phone number:

Name of supervisor:

Your Job title:

Your job description:

Dates of employment: from_____ to_____
(Mo., day, year)

Special recognition at job:

Reason you are no longer at this job:

GUIDE TO LOCAL LAS VEGAS RESOURCES.

WELFARE DIVISION OFFICE

—Assists in basic needs through cash grants, food stamps, medical assistance, employment and training and securing child support.

700 Belrose St, Las Vegas. 486-5000

- State welfare – food stamps, help organization
 486-5040
- Moms program...486-5268

3700 E. Charleston Blvd, Las Vegas. 486-5000

1040 W. Owens Ave, Las Vegas. 486-5040

538-A S. Boulder Hwy, Henderson. 486-5000

Canon Senior Center, 340 N. Eleventh St, Ste.103, Las Vegas.
....486-3600

Lowden Center, 3333 Cambridge St, Las Vegas............486-8274

Professional Development Center, 701 N. Rancho, Las Vegas.
....486-5000

4130 E. Desert Inn Road, Las Vegas (Child Support)
....486-8500

MEDICAL ASSISTANCE

Clark County health District,..........................**625 Shadow Ln.**
....385-1291

- (Family planning – sliding scale; immunizations – free ; Healthy Kids – Medicaid. 8:00 a.m.-4:00 p.m. with Medicaid pending slip).
- Health Card. 383-3271

Clark County Social Service, ...**1600 Pinto Ln.**
....455-4270

- Mediation service with respect to disputes/disagreement.
- Help organization, rental and mortgage payments as well as utility assistance(only one month)
- Mediation service with respect to disputes/disagreements.
 455-3898

1058 W. Owens Ave..455-7208

- Medical assistance for those not eligible for State of Nevada Medicaid or Homemaker Program.
- Assistance with rent for pending Temporary Assistance to Needy Families (TANF) clients. Also has
- GATE Program for able–bodied adults. In return for work for the county, individual or family gets assistance with rent in form of check or a voucher issued by Clark County Social Service.
- Rental payments and mortgage (one month only) and utility assistance. Should bring eviction notice, proof of income, other bill, ID and all other relevant paperwork.

Community Health Center, ...**916 W. Owens Ave.**
.. ..631-8800

- Sliding scale, walk–ins accepted; pregnancy testing .
- AFAN(Aid for AIDS of Nevada).
 648-0177

Epicenter, ...**2100 S. Maryland Pkwy, Ste.5**.
....732-8776

- Medical & dental assistance for client 12-18 who are not Medicaid eligible and have no other nsurance. Attention Deficit Disorder evaluation & treatment for ages 2-18. Well–baby exams for ages 0-4.

UNIVERSITY MEDICAL CENTER

Emergency Room ....1800 W. Charleston Blvd, ...383-2000

- Emergency medical care.
- Outpatient clinics – adult patients (Shadow lane / Charleston) 383-2631
- Pediatric patients (Ste.303 in UMC Pediatric & Trauma Center) 383-3642

St. Vincent's Catholic Comm. Svcs, Shelter....................**1501 N. Las Vegas Blvd.** 384-0409

- Help organization 385-2550
- Catholic Charities of Southern Nevada,(St. Vincent's Dining Hall) 385-7801
- Lunch service is 12:00noon-1:00p.m for homeless. Dinner service is from 4:00p.m- 5:30p.m.
  Only for those in approved program, i.e., Shade tree. Can assist with other necessities.
- Food Pantry: Monday 8:00a.m-5:00p.m, Tuesday-Friday 8:00a.m-3:00p.m, bring ID on everyone in household and proof of residency (i.e., rent receipt or utility bill).
- Rent assistance (rental payment-one month only, motel stays)& clothing 383-0766
- Clothing, need rent receipt and social security cards for all family members as well as picture ID for the head of household.
- M.A.S.H (Mobilized Assistance Shelter for the homeless) 229-4806

FINANCIAL ASSISTANCE

Consumer Credit Counseling Service of Southern Nevada, 3650 S. Decatur, Ste.30. 364-0344

- Free counseling, assistance with debt management plans and classes on money management.

Social Security administration, general information phone number..(800) 772-1213

5460 W. Sahara Ave...248-8717
1820 E. Lake Mead Blvd, N. Las V 649-1982
2225 Civic Center Dr....649-1982
State Industrial Insurance System,..........**1700 W. Charleston Blvd**
....388-1000

- For information about filing on–the–job accident claims.
- Help organization,
 388-3100

MICS. HELP NUMBERS

SHORT–TERM EMPLOYMENT.

Employment security DIV., casual labor, 1001 A Street.
....486-3441

MEAL AND/OR SHELTER.

St Vincents,................................**1501 N. Main St, Las Vegas**
....385-7801
Las Vegas Rescue Mission,..........**414-480 W. Bonanza, Las Vegas.**
....382-1766
Salvation Army......................…......**35 W. Owens, Las Vegas.**
....649-8240

- Assistance with past due utility bills only when funds are available.
  They cannot help with deposits or turn-on fees.
- For shelter
 639-0277
- Food assistance (door open for dinner from 3:00p.m. to 3:30p.m)
 649-7638
- 2900 Palomino Lane, Las Vegas (varies according to program & needs
  served)..870-4430

Term Assist. Domestic Crisis Mash ....**1581 N. Main or 1559
Main St, Las Vegas**..388-0088

- Crisis intervention program. Federal, state, county and city agencies
  have representatives here to help with families in crisis. Must be
  screened here to get into the M.A.S.H village.
 229-4806

Safe House, ……………...…………….. **18 Sunrise Drive, suite G70, Henderson, NV 89014.** …………………………………………...415-7203

- (Victims of domestic violence & abuse –woman's shelter).

Shade Tree. …………………………….**1 W. Owens Ave, N. Las Vegas.** …………………………………………………………………....385-0072

- (Cannot be under the influence of alcohol or drugs. Must be able to care for self –woman's shelter)

Cambridge Family Resources. ………**3827 S. Maryland Pkwy, Las Vegas** …………………………………………………...455-7386
City Mission of Las Vegas. …………...**1118 Fremont St, Las Vegas.** …………………………………………………………...384-1930

- (Social security number, ID Card and Express a need).

Greater Las Vegas – Family Resources Center...1200 N. Eastern Ave, NV 89101 …………………………………………………..657-6762
Catholic Charities of Southern Nevada. ………**808 S. Main St, Las Vegas.** ……………………………………………………….385-2662

LICENSES AND CERTIFICATIONS

Sherrif's Card. ………………………….…... **601 E. Fremont, Las Vegas.** …………………………………………………....229-3306
Tam Card. ………………………………..…………**CALL FOR DATE** …………………………………………………………...647-1954
Driver's License Info. …....……………………….**2701 E. Sahara (FULL SERV)**……....…………………………………………486-4368

4021 W. Carey (FULL SERV)
8250 W. Flamingo (FULL SERV)
4110 Donovan (FULL SERV)
1399 American Pacific (HND)

HELP ORGANIZATIONS

AARP………………………...……………… **330 W. Washington, #10.** ………………………………………………………...648-3356

American Red Cross ....…... 1819 E. Charleston,
....791-3311
CCSN Re-entry Center ....3200 E. Cheyenne,
....651-4332
Charleston Outlet Thrift Store ....1548 E. Charleston,
....388-1446
Deputy Commissioner –Vets ....…...1700 Vegas Drive,
....636-3070
Gov Commission of Handicapped ....555 E. Washington,
....486-2750
Help of Southern Nevada ....3909 Maryland Pkwy, #205.
....369-4357
Jewish Family Service ....1555 E. Flamingo,
....732-0304
Labor Commission ....555 E. Washington, #1400.
....486-2650
Nevada Business Service ....….....930 W. Owens Ave.
....647-4929
Nevada Legal Service ....701 W. Lake Mead.
....399-5627
SR-Citizen Info-Referral ....953 E. Sahara.
....382-4357
Small Business Administration ....…............301 Stewart,
....388-6611
State Rehabilitation ....…..628 Belrose,
....486-5230
VA Outpatient Clinic ....…....1700 Vegas Drive,
....636-3000
VA Regional Office (Reno) ....1201 Terminal Way.
....1-800-827-1000
Veterans Outreach Center ....1040 E. Sahara, Ste.1.
....388-6268

OTHER STATE OF NEVADA VETERAN JOB SERVICE OFFICE

3405 South Maryland Parkway, North Las Vegas, NV 89030
2827 Las Vegas Blvd, North Las Vegas, NV 89106702-486-0111.
902 West Owens, Las Vegas, NV 89019, 702-486-0211,   702-486-5300

NOTE : All offices have computers for public use, fax machines, telephone, photocopiers and resume information. FREE.

FAMILY PLANNING CLINIC

Economic Opportunity Board (EOB).............**2224 Comstock Dr.** 647-3319

Trinity Counseling Center..........................**968 E. Sahara Ave.** 731-6240

- (Marriage & family therapist)

Compass Counseling Center ....**2685 S. Rainbow Blvd.** 253-6510

- (Marriage & family therapist)

LEGAL ASSISTANCE

Clark County Pro Bono Project. ....**701 E. Bridger, Ste. 101.** 783-3113

- (Nevada legal service)
  ....386-1070 or 1-800-522-1070

- Family court matters to include advice on: filing of restraining order, child support, divorce, help combating domestic violence and child abuse. Emancipation of 16-years-old minor and older. Sealing of criminal records to obtain employment and voting rights.

Nevada Disability Advocacy & Law Center. ....**6039 Eldora Ave, Ste. C- Box 3**..257-8150
Safe Nest. Confidential. ....877-0133 / 646-4981

MISCELLANEOUS RESOURCES

AFAN(Aid for AIDS of Nevada) ....**230 S. Rancho, Ste.211,** 382-2326
Help of Southern Nevada ....**953 E. Sahara Ave,**
Ste.23B/ 35B208..369-HELP (4357)

- Weatherization Program, displaced homemaker, information and referral service, employment assistance including bus tokens and gas vouchers.

Las Vegas Indian Center ....**2300 W. Bonanza Rd,**
....647-5842

- Job placement, GED program, AA meetings and substance abuse, Indian child welfare program, potluck dinner on the first Saturday of each month. Must have proof of heritage; if not, they will help to track heritage. They also provide a heritage tracking class, and rental.

Nevada Association for the Handicapped ......**6200 W. Oakey Blvd.**
....870-7050
Opportunity Village ....…......**6300 W. Oakey Blvd.**
....…..........259-3700

- Assistance to mentally challenged and mentally handicapped.

Poor People Pulling Together ....**1881 N. "J" St.**
....…......648-4645

- Provides help to save clients' homes through HUD and Wells Fargo Bank. Also help with remodeling, food, clothing and linens.

Runaway Youth Hotline (Westcare) ....**401 Martin Luther King Blvd.** ....…..............................…..................385-3335
Veteran's Affairs, Dept. of ..…...........**3233 W. Charleston Blvd.**
....…..................1-800-827-1000

- Benefits information and assistance.

COUNSELING / SUPPORT GROUPS

Bridge Counseling ....…....**1701 W. Charleston Blvd, Ste. 300.**
....…........474-6450

- Sliding scale, requires appointment, 9:00 a.m.–8:00 p.m., Monday – Friday, 8:00 a.m-3:00 p.m., Saturday.

Children's Behavioral Service ....**6171 W. Charleston Blvd.**
....…..........486-6100
Community Counseling Center ....…....**1120 Almond Tree Ln.**
....…..........369-8700
Counseling Center of Southern Nevada .....**909 E. Bonneville Ave.**
....384-8362

- Sliding scale, appointment required.

Las Vegas Mental Health Center ....**6161 W. Charleston Blvd.**
....486-6000
Mojave mental Health ....**3171 S. Jones Blvd.**
....253-0818

- Accepts Medicaid.

Special Children's Clinic ....**1161 S. Valley View Blvd.**
....486-7670

- Developmentally delayed children ages 0-3 years.

CRISIS HOTLINE

Children's Resource Bureau
....486-7650 / 486-7635

- 8:00 a.m.– 5:00 p.m., Monday –Friday. Emotional crises, suicide, abuse of youths and families.

Community Action Against Rape ......**749 Veteran's Memorial Dr**.
....385-2153 / 366-1640

- Rape crisis center.

S.A.S.E (Sexual Abuse Survivors Evolving).
....432-9100
Safest (formerly T.A.D.C), ...**3441 W. Sahara Ave. #C3.**
....646-4981 / 877-0133
Suicide Prevention Center
....731-2990

EMPLOYMENT AND TRAINING SERVICE

Community College of Southern Nevada ....**3200 E. Cheyenne Ave.** 651-4000

- (Admissions ext. 4060, re-entry ext. 4332)

Clark County School District, Adult Education. ...**2701 E. St. Louis Ave.** 799-8650
Nevada Employment Security.........................**Job Information Hotline**...225-2200

135 S. 8th St..486-3300
2827 N. Las Vegas Blvd, N. Las Vegas......................486-5600
119 Water St, Henderson.......................................486-6710

Nevada State Welfare Division Office ....**538A S. Boulder
Hwy, Henderson** 486-1224

FOOD ASSISTANCE

FISH Emergency Assistance
....735-0300

- Call and they will direct you to one of their six local food banks. You are limited to one visit every six weeks.

Las Vegas Rescue Mission ....**608 –610 N. "E" St.**
....382-9344 / 382-1766

- Dinner served at 5:00 p.m. Free clothing for women and children 9:00-10:00 a.m. on Thursdays and sometimes on Saturdays. Free clothing for men on Thursdays 5:00-6:00 p.m. No voucher required
- For Shelter (women and children stay separate from the men; women and children must report in by 5:00p.m. for intake into the women's shelter. Men interviewed for intake in transient food line from 4:00-6:00p.m. No phone interview
 382-5924

Christ Church Episcopal. ....**2000 S. Maryland Pkwy.** 735-5437

- Food (must be referral from Help of So Nev.)

RENT ASSISTANCE

- All recipients must have the means to pay next month's rent if assistance is granted.
- Current inability to pay must be the result of an unforeseen event.

E.O.B Project Home ....**330 W. Washington, Ste. 7** .
....647-3307

- Rental payment (up to one month's rent to prevent homeless or 1st month's rent and deposit to end homelessness). Application taken Wednesday at 8:00 a.m. or Monday afternoon at M.A.S.H Crisis Intervention at **1501 N. Las Vegas Blvd**.

Lutheran Social Ministry ....**580 E. St. Louis Ave.**
....734-7088

- Rental & utility payments (one month only). There must be at least one minor child.

Salvation Army ....**830 E. Lake Mead Dr, Henderson.**
....565-9578

- Rental and utility assistance for zip code 89122, 89014, 89015 and 89016 **ONLY**.

HOUSING

Clark County Housing Authority ....**5390 E. Flamingo Rd.**
....541-8041
Golden Rainbow ....**1170 S. Martin Luther King Blvd.** 384-2899

- Low cost housing for people with HIV&AIDS. Financial assistance with rent, utilities and medical bills. Support and counseling services, if desired. Screened and referred by Aid for AIDS of Nevada (AFAN) (see listing under miscellaneous resources).

Housing and Urban Development ....**333 E. Rancho. Ste, 700.** 388-6776

- Subsidized apartment

Las Vegas City Housing Authority ....**420 N. 10th St.**
....386-2727
Nevada Homes for Youth ....**525 S. 13th St.**
....380-2889

- Affordable housing for middle to low income families. Independent living for minor, mostly through court order, county or state Division of Child and Family Service (DCFS).

North Las Vegas Housing Authority ....**1632 Yale St, N. Las Vegas**...649-2451
Parson's Place ....**624 E. Steward** 383-0847

- Transitional housing for single men, women and couple with out children recently released from a shelter, correctional facility or rehabilitation.

Women's Development Center ....**953 E. Sahara Ave. # 201.**
....**796-7770**

- Transitional housing program. For single parents with children willing to work full-time or work part-time and go to school part-time. Client should provide eviction notice and ID for all family.

SHELTERS

Crossroads/Marian Residence ....…..............**1526 N. Main St.**
....**385-2777**

- For men and women 50-70 years of age who have recently experienced a traumatic life event (i.e., death of spouse, etc.) that jeopardizes their ability to live independently. Screened by social security staff on the premises.

IHN–Interfaith Hospitality Network
(Shelter for families. Call for intake.) **638-8806**

Shade Tree Shelter..................................…..……**1560 N. Main St.**
....…....**385-4596**

- Shelter for women with children or single women. Sign in is by 3:30p.m.

CHILD CARE

Economic Opportunity Board of Clark County..........**708 S. 6th St.**
....…..........**387-1872**

- Child care assistance, Headstart Center. WIC.

Head Start–Economic Opportunity Board ....**2228 Comstock Dr**. **387-5579**

- Provides preschool education to children from low-income families and seeks to enhance the children's family's educational, nutritional, psychological and health potential through 14 preschool centers.

Holy Family Day Care (sliding scale & child care)...........**451 E. Twain Ave**. **735-4358**

Nevada Association of Latin Americans (NALA) Pre-school and Child Care Center. ....**323 N. Maryland Pkwy.** 382-6252

CLOTHING

Crisis Pregnancy Center.............................**721 E. Charleston Blvd.** ....366-1247 or 366-0764

- Free maternity and baby clothes only (up to children's size 5). Also diaper, formula, peer counseling and pregnancy testing. By appointment only. No voucher required..

Desert Industries Thrift Store ....**1300 N. Las Vegas Blvd.** 649-8191

- Must have a referral from an LDS Bishop. Assistance is free with referral and client does not have to be LDS. This is geared toward those deficient in basic life and work skills.
- Furniture and appliances may also be available.

Faith Lutheran ....**707 N. Rancho St.** 646-5668

- One free change of clothing with agency referral in letterhead. List all names and ages.
- Free clothing for women and children 9:00-10:00a.m. on Thursdays and sometimes on Saturdays.

Jr. League Repeat Boutique.............................**1040 E. Twain** 731-2446

- Free but must have a referral from HELP of Southern Nevada (369-HELP).

Martin's Thrift Shop.....................................**1219 S. Main St.** 382-9344

- One free change of clothing (requires proof of assistance, i.e., referral with names, ages and social security number).

Opportunity Village Thrift Store. ....**921 S. Main St.** 383-1082
538 S. Boulder Hwy. 564-7128

Salvation Army Thrift Store...........................**801 N. Lamb Blvd**.
....438-8017
4001 W. Charleston Blvd. 878-8022
5200 Boulder Hwy. 456-7593
2035 Yale St, N. Las Vegas. 642-3811
471 Boulder Hwy, Henderson. 565-6071

- Some free clothing with referral from Salvation Army Shelter, Salvation Army Family
- Assistance also helps two families on Tuesdays and Fridays with food bags and clothing.

St. Jude's Good Buy Thrift Shop............**171 E. Charleston Blvd**.
....386-0772

PREGNANCY TESTING CENTER

- (Check address at Medical Assistance, Pregnancy Center under 'Clothing'.)

Economic Opportunity Board. ....**5B Tonopah Ave, N.
Las Vegas**. 649-4272
750 Major St, Henderson 565-8443

- By appointment only, 8:00a.m.-12:00 noon and 1:00 p.m.-5:00 p.m., Medicaid accepted.

Huntridge Teen Clinic. ....**2100 S. Maryland Pkwy,
Ste. 5**. 732-8776

- Phone number is voice mail number. Call and leave a message and your call will be returned.
- Free pregnancy tests are given to young women 12-18 years old.

Lifeline Pregnancy Assistance. ....**1800 S. Industrial Rd**.
....871-6585

- Free pregnancy testing, no appointment required, 9:00 a.m.-3:30 p.m. requires picture ID.
- Also provides assistance with clothing, food and parenting class.

North Las Vegas Public Health Center. ....**3262 A Civic Center**
....642-3525

- No appointment needed, 8:00 a.m.-4:00 p.m. pending slip or Medicaid accept.

PRENATAL, NUTRITION PROGRAMS

Baby Your Baby. 1-800-429-2669

- Referral for State of Nevada Medicaid clients with respect to prenatal care, nutrition and other pregnancy issues. Local programs are:

- **Baby Steps Prenatal Program** 1-800-670-7890
- **Lake Mead Hospital Pregnancy Center.** 675-5510
- **Sunrise Pregnancy Center.** 735-2229

W.I.C (Women, Infants and Children) ....**12 location.**
call for information..1-800-463-8942
Family Cabinet ....**300 W. Boston Ave.**
....385-5437

- Referral service for prenatal classes and counseling.
- (Nevada State Welfare).

TRANSPORTATION

Citizens Area Transit (CAT)
....455-7433
Economic Opportunity Board of Clark County (EOB)........800 W.
Bonanza Rd. 646-2062

- 55 years or older. Not available in Henderson or Boulder City. $3 one way/$5 round trip.
- Reservations can be made 1-14 days in advance. Service is first come, first served.

Medicaid Clients Only (Assistance is getting to and from medical appointment only)...486-5269
Help of Southern Nevada (bus tokens and gas voucher for job searches and interview)...369-HELP(4357)

UTILITY ASSISTANCE

- (check at Medical Assistance-Clark County Social Security and Catholic Charities, Lutheran Social Ministries and Salvation Army at Rental Assistance and Salvation Army at Meal/Shelter).

Nevada Power Assis-
tance...367-5555

- Contact for information on how to apply for Low Income home Energy Assistance (LIHEA) and Energy Crisis Intervention Program (ECIP) or call the State Directly at 486-3000, ext. 4420 or 1-800-992-0900, ext. 4420.

Giving Life Ministries ....**416 Perlite Wy,**
Henderson..**565-4984**

About the Author

Robert Saunders is a New York City businessman/entrepreneur who moved to Las Vegas in 1996, after purchasing a major Las Vegas enterprise, to act as CEO/President. When the business was sold in 1998 he stayed in Las Vegas and became the Director of Special Employment Services, a non-profit corporation that specializes in finding employment for individuals with disabilities. This position has allowed him to utilize his extensive business experience as a bridge between those needing work and those looking for workers. He considers it a unique opportunity to give something of day-to-day value to the Las Vegas community.

He has previously written a Survival Manual for Physically Abused Women and essays on racial and human conditions in modern times.

Printed in the United States
93321LV00008B/18/A